Giggles and Tears

Sigi

Giggles and Tears by Sigi

Copyright © 2020 SIGI

Giggles and Tears

Perspective Press Global Ltd

All rights reserved.

ISBN: 978-1-8380044-2-2

"The future belongs to those who believe in the beauty of their dreams."

Eleanor Roosevelt

RANDOM ASSORTMENT OF THOUGHTS

Giggles and Tears by Sigi

I can feel the darkness
As it creeps upon my skin
I can feel the anger
That is coming from within
It's directed towards
All the things I didn't say
Telling me that even now
It still isn't too late
It's directed towards
All the things I didn't do
When I could have done something
Whenever I wanted to
This anger has crawled
Its way out of my heart
It will explode as a supernova
And everyone will feel its spark
But as anger leaves my soul
I feel a peace I've never felt
And in its place I can see growing
An emotion I've never had
It is love and self-fulfillment
When you accept just who you are
And don't let others try to shape you
Cause you were made to be bizarre
And when I realize that it was anger
That had stopped me all along
I find out love can make you stronger
Those who deny it are just wrong
For all my days and nights before
I had felt so incomplete
But now I'm living my life fully
At the tempo of my heartbeat

THE RAIN

Giggles and Tears by Sigi

The rain drips down the umbrella
As I walk with my head down to the ground
Splashing footsteps give me company
Since I don't bother to look around

As my head raises towards the sky
I feel the water down on my face
In that moment I think the rain
Asks if I need something to erase

I think about all of the memories
That I have made in my young life
And there are lots and lots of them
I want to cut down with a knife

I think about my deep regrets
About the things I did not say
And all the thoughts that I withheld
'Till it became too late a day

I think about the good I did
And all the mistakes I ever made
As if they could cancel each other out
If I just put them on a balance plate

And I begged and begged the rain:
"Please wash away all those bad dreams"
But then it whispered in my ear
"Nothing is ever as bad as it seems"

STAY

Giggles and Tears by Sigi

Tell me your desires
When we sit alone at night
Tell me your secrets
Let the moon shine them bright

Let me know all about your wishes
What makes you look forward not back
Confess to me all your hopes and dreams
Whisper them while breathing down my neck

Let's talk about the big things
Not those we won't remember
So we both don't bury the memory
Of this warm night in September

For all the victories I've had
You are the one I hold most dear
And I'm so very grateful to you
For not destroying us with your fear

Know I'll always be here for you
With no hesitation I will
And whatever may come in our way
I know that we'll overcome it, we will

'Cause darling, my love for you is so grand
That it won't ever fade away
So since we only have one life
Come here by my side and stay

THAT ONE

You think you know her,
But from the truth that's too far,
She keeps herself hidden away,
Locked in the prison she calls her heart.

She's built a fortress around her,
That not many can pass through,
But there's a small locked door in there,
Whose key she has given to you.

That key lies in the thoughts she has gifted,
In the words she spoke with her eyes,
In the memories she once mentioned so quickly,
It lies in her silence-filled cries.

There's no one that thinks she's strong,
"Her kindness makes her weak" they say,
But they forget without her smile,
They might not have lasted another day.

So when you do find her key,
And that, love, I'm sure you'll do,
Open her door, admire her kingdom,
And in her never-ending garden...plant a flower or two.

HOPE

May your path be lightened,
'Cause I know your fear of the dark,
And remember even in your worst times,
Something good is about to start.

May you always be kind,
For it's not only you who has a heart,
And if you're not careful enough,
You might break someone else's apart.

May you carry love in your life,
Someone, to let down a rope,
So when you feel like you're drowning,
You may always have a little hope.

TO MY FUTURE CHILD

If you want to,
The world is yours.
For sure, you'll have me by your side,
I'll help you open doors and lights.

I'll teach you the good things,
And the bad ones too,
'Cause there's a thin wall between them,
Which can only be built by you.

I'll show you how to love,
Make you feel like a better person dear,
Do you understand what I'm saying?
Tell me, darling, do you hear?.

But most of all my baby,
Hope is what I'll teach,
For when you're near the ending,
You'll rise back on your feet.

I CAME

Giggles and Tears by Sigi

I believe in second chances,
In the universe's way of saying it's right,
I believe that despite our different lives,
We're equals under the same stars at night.

I believe in one's strong will,
To make things that are worth it happen,
I believe that you haven't fully lived,
If you haven't changed at least once your direction.

I believe in the good hearts,
In the ones whose world they change,
I believe in all this beauty,
That, without notice, comes with age.

Perhaps, my naivety will fade as I grow old,
And my beliefs won't be the same,
But the one thing I know for sure,

Is before conquering, I came.

THOUGHTS

Lies all around me,
Don't quite know what to believe,
And I wonder what the hell,
What are they trying to achieve?

Trust is stumbling down the dark alleys,
It seems to have lost its way,
Indecisiveness has conquered me,
Should I leave or should I stay.

Life obviously has no mercy,
And I know now that's a fact,
But it's in our hands to decide,
If we wanna be alive or dead.

REGRETS

Someday I wish we hadn't met,
And that this ache I could forget,
It's unexplainable, with no reason why,
Thinking of you brings water to my eyes.

There's nothing left for me to say,
I'm sorry I've realised too late,
That without you it's hard to live,
And for that, myself I can't forgive.

It doesn't matter whose fault it was,
Who thought too little, or who too much,
Because it's the end that defined,
Whose feelings lasted and who didn't mind.

And if I could just look into those eyes again,
I would remember exactly why I'd ran,
Because that blue I drowned in so deep,
Made me forget the life I could seek.

WHEN

Giggles and Tears by Sigi

When the night feels endless and dead,
When it feels like no one's alive,
Remember it only takes a few hours,
Before the whole world starts to thrive.

When you feel like your battles are lost,
When there's nothing left to fight for,
Don't forget making peace with your demons,
Is more important than declaring them war.

When your tears start falling continuously,
And your happiness is washed away by the sea,
You should know that letting people in makes it easier,
And to the door, my darling, you hold the key.

But who am I to tell you what will happen,
Who's gonna accept you and who won't,
After all, I'm just a girl
Who your memory forever will haunt.

And just because I'm a part of your past,
Not your present anymore,
It doesn't mean I won't share your future,
It doesn't mean I'll never be yours.

So I'm telling you this right now,
When you feel like you're all alone,
Stop thinking and imagine me there,
Standing with you heart and bone.

LEFT

Giggles and Tears by Sigi

I came and I went,
Never stayed in one place,
Always having something to do,
Always speeding my pace.

And I never stayed anywhere,
Or with anyone at all,
So be prepared to lose me,
Before you even have me whole.

I promise to disappoint you,
Make you regret you ever met me,
But I only ask one thing,
Don't forget our estranged history.

Whatever your heart may tell you,
Wherever it may lie,
When I leave, remember,
For me, you needn't cry.

All that I am now,
Is nothing that you knew,
And I want to believe that someday,
You'll meet the new me, too.

But I can't have hope for something,
That depended on your actions and mine,
So instead I'll do what I do best,

And without words, say my goodbyes.

SHE

Giggles and Tears by Sigi

She was born to move the mountains,
To raise the rivers from their beds,
She was born to make their world shake,
When her name popped in their heads.
She was born to follow sea storms,
Not stay in the dry old land,
She was born to be imperfectly real,
And never needed to pretend.
But when the world started a war,
All together against her,
She couldn't fight them, so gave up,
And inside her bed she curled.
Because people want the sun,
And the calm sea with no waves,
They cannot see the beauty,
That in front of them, lays.
But deep inside she knew,
She wasn't made for this world,
She didn't want some paper,
To determine what's her worth.
She didn't want a comfort,
That only made her sad,
She wanted love and happiness,
Things (and people) that made her so mad.
And one day she understood,
She didn't need to stay and fight,
So she got up at 2 AM,
And left before the end of the night.
She went wherever her feet did,
Never stopped to think about the past,
Because she knew a truth known only by a few,
That nothing ever really lasts.
She found the joy of creating,
Of caring deeply for your own,

Of loving unconditionally,
With both her heart and her 206 bones.
She was born to move the mountains,
To raise the rivers from their beds,
She was born to make their world shake,
When her name popped in their heads.

DUST

Giggles and Tears by Sigi

I never believed in myself,
And neither did they, as well,
I saw it in their pitiful eyes,
And only from that, I could tell:
The world felt sorry for me,
It thought I was made out of powder,
It said I could crumble so easily,
If they just screamed a little bit louder.
How I found humor in those thoughts,
How those prejudices made me laugh,
They think I am so damn fragile,
That I could easily be cut in half.
And yes, I do tell people too much,
And yes, I look at myself in the mirror and stare,
Yes, I know how good it feels to be accepted,
That's exactly why I let myself care.
But don't you ever underestimate my strength,
Don't you ever think I can turn into dust,
Don't you ever think I'll forgive you,
If you've just so much as broken my trust.
I'll admit that my emotions come in rogue waves,
And my anger, falls down like a winter storm,
But my mind is a constellation of galaxies,
And my heart, the sun, as big and as warm.
So when the world knocks at my door so loudly,
And tells me: " You never will fit.",
I'll say: "The world shouldn't feel sorry about me,
Instead, I ought to feel sorry 'bout it."

THAT CITY

Giggles and Tears by Sigi

I know not of Paris,
I know not of L.A,
Though I've always longed,
To visit them, and stay.
I know not of Asia,
Neither do I of Africa,
I've never been to Australia,
I've never stepped foot in America.
There are so many places,
That I haven't yet been,
And there are so many people,
That I haven't yet seen.
But I once went to a place,
Where I felt I could be anything,
I felt such an undeniable freedom,
That only that place could bring.
As I walked through it I noticed,
That a singular smile wouldn't leave my face,
I never thought I'd be so happy,
When I first said: "Oh, I've been to that place."
I saw its most wonderful beauties,
I felt it in the summer heat,
That city caught me by surprise,
And it simply swept me off my feet.
I smiled at every person that I saw,
They felt like people from another time,
But in those moments I couldn't see,
The difference between who were they and who was I.
I sat in sweat-filled subway trains,
I used the tramways everyday,
I saw from its red buses,
How the skies were never gray.
My mind wasn't prepared for that,
I never knew how you could love a city,

And it wasn't just because of its views,
It wasn't just because it was pretty.

It was because of its crowded streets,
Of that fulfillment when you wandered there,
Of that adrenaline of busy people,
That felt like you didn't have any time to stop and stare.
So if they ask me where,
Where do I see myself in a few years,
I'll say: "London, United Kingdom"
And that's the only sure thing they'll hear.

THE GIRL IN MY DREAMS

I am awoken by raindrop sounds on my window,
I don't hear the alarm clock.
I get up, stare at the mirror,
That girl, in my dreams, is staring back.

She hasn't woken up yet.
She sleepwalks into the bathroom,
and then back to her closet.
Dresses up, gives her mom a kiss,
Brushes a strand of messy hair off her face.
Going to school, catching up with friends,
It all seems like a routine now.
It's just what happens when I'm not asleep.
She comes back home,
Finishes her homework,
Chats with her brother.
He wants to show her his inventions,
She doesn't have the time.
She greets her parents,
when *they* come from work.
When the time comes to sleep,
She turns off the light,
And closes her eyes.
I'm awake now.

THEY

A challenge like no other,
Her soul was for him,
He couldn't understand how easily,
She could get under his skin.
They disagreed on everything,
Could never find a common ground,
Though they both knew no matter what,
Their love was as true as the earth is round.
But, as life went on and on,
And other things got in their way,
They wished they could argue about silly things,
Even just for another day.
Choosing different paths was hard,
As he went to follow his dream,
She stayed to take care of her own,
All the time waiting for him.
One day, she got a letter from him,
Which made her break down on the floor,
He cared about somebody else now,
He didn't love her anymore.
As the months passed, she had forgotten,
How much he'd meant to her,
She could now only remember,
The huge mess they once were.
Whereas on the other side of the world,
He saw her smile in another's face,
But he missed her hazel eyes that shone,
Whenever she would stare into space.
After a very long time,
He went back to see his land,
And when he saw her he couldn't believe,
That finally in front of him she stands.

Giggles and Tears by Sigi

They cried and laughed and shared so much stories,
And during this time they both realized a thing,
Despite living different lives,
They still could pull at each other's heart strings.

I DO CARE

You make me laugh when I want to cry
You make me live when I want to die
You're always there when I need you to be
Helping me rise back on my feet

We're still young but somehow I'm sure
Ours is a love so true and pure
And no matter how much they taunt
I have known since forever who I actually want

And though I've always held back
It was because of the bravery that I lack
But no more fear, no more overthinking
I am going to follow my heart without so much as blinking

I know deep down I'm doing the right thing
Because I've seen the joy loving someone can bring
I have seen the solace found when you let someone in
I have seen the excitement when they get under your skin

But I have never really felt these types of feelings
I have never reached high enough to touch your ceiling
I have never let somebody I like think that I care
But for you, my darling, know I'll always be there.

TONIGHT

Tonight calm descends upon my house,
While my head rests warmly on my pillow,
As I listen oh so closely,
To the raindrops trickling down my window.

I wish I could go outside,
And let the wind make a mess out of my hair,
It's cold and stormy but now,
Not in the least would I care.

Thoughts are swirling in my mind,
And I'm struggling to get a grasp,
It seems like everybody I know,
Doesn't see me but my mask.

There is some crack inside of me,
That I can't figure out how to fill,
It feels as if I'm pushing a huge invisible rock,
Up a big never-ending hill.

I HOPE

15 years ago, my mom gave birth to a baby girl,
She had big green eyes, that would later become the color of honey,
And those curious eyes, they looked at everything, seeing right through.
And that baby...
That baby was me.
And I grew,
Overly emotional, not having a care in the world about what others thought,
The blurred line between my heart and mind, almost seemed to not exist at all.
If you gave me a song to listen to,
I would learn to sing it with every atom of my being
If you gave me paper,
I'd turn it into a poem that would make your eyes become clouds exploding with rain. Because, I knew that, words matter. They can change or break you.
And still, there are a lot of things I don't know
Maybe when I do, I'll change or break overnight myself,
But I have people that will love me no matter what and for that, I'm eternally GRATEFUL
Life hasn't taught me lessons yet,
It hasn't beaten me up enough so that I can't get back on my feet,
But when it does, I hope that someone will give me their hand.
My eyes shine if I talk about something I love,
And when I do, I hope that somebody's listening
Because there's so much of my words begging to be heard out there,
Though today my smile seems to be stuck in my face,

I hope that when my nose is red,
My eyes swollen and my voice is breaking,
I'll find solace on the beauty of the way the stars have painted themselves on the night sky I hope that someday my lungs will breathe the air I've been searching for,
And I'll make a home there, where every heartbreak slipped under its door,
Is slipped back outside like an envelope, unopened.
Because then, the light in the heart is the only thing I will desire.
Now, in my young life, I haven't had the chance to see the world, yet
And I don't know if I'm powerful enough to ever make a change in it.
But I hope that, one day, maybe I will.

TO MY LITTLE BIRD

Fly away little bird,
You are ready now,
Though I'm not ready to let you go,
I have to, somehow.

Fly away into the world,
Make some friends and memories too,
Flap your wings for as long as you can,
Fly over every ocean's blue.

Listen to the beats of your little heart,
Put them in harmony with your song,
Find a birdie to hold on to,
When everything goes wrong.

Be free little bird,
It's time you got out of your nest,
It's time you had a family of your own,
And go into that knotty quest.

But, don't worry little bird,
I'll always be here when you're down,
My arms will be wide open,
Anytime you think you'll drown.

TO MY MOM

Giggles and Tears by Sigi

This is for my mom,
On the 5th of May,
I am writing you this poem,
Because there are some things I wanted to say:

Thank you for teaching me right,
And for always giving me love,
Thank you for being a mom,
I can bravely say I am proud of,
Thanks for lending me an ear,
Each time I needed to talk,
And always giving me a shoulder,
Thank you for being my rock,

You are all I wish to be,
Here's what you made MOTHER mean to me:

Making time,
Opening all my doors,
Taking care of me,
Helping me stand when I fall to the floor.
Embodying me everyday,
Reminding me you're here to stay.

I love you mom,
To the moon and back,
I love when you manage,
A smile out of me to crack.
And though you can't really choose your mom,
If that was something I had to do,
Just know that no matter what,
My choice would *always, always* be **you**.

HOW MUCH

"How much do I have?" I asked the time,
When I was as small as a flower,
"You have all the time in the world," She said,
"You don't need me to give you some extra hours"

"How much do I have?" I asked the time,
When my voice became loud and strong,
" You needn't worry," She said,
"For your days here are still long."

"How much do I have now?" I asked the time,
When my hair turned into a bundle of gray,
"You don't have as much as you did before," She said,
"But for a while you still can stay."

"How much?" I asked the time,
When my bones were old and I knew I would soon sleep,
"I'm sorry dear, but not very long," She told me,
"And now, an extra hour, is the most you can keep."

BIG HOUSES

What does it matter if we have big houses,
With columns and big ceilings, too,
When we have this beautiful nature,
That everyone is free to view.

What does it matter if we own a pool,
When we have the ocean where we can swim all day,
When we have the bittersweet salt,
Instead of the drowning chlorine that so heavily can weigh.

What does it matter if we've paper-like flowers,
And trees that aren't true and green,
When we can walk in the wonderful forest,
And suck in that breathtaking scene.

There's no importance, I dare to say,
To all these human-made artificialities here,
When we have such wonderful landscapes,
That are as old as this sphere.

MAYBE

Maybe we weren't meant for this world,
But for another altogether,
Maybe our souls couldn't be hurled,
Without being destroyed forever.

Maybe waiting on a face,
Is driving in an endless highway,
Where you can't decide to speed up the pace,
Or rather take a turn and drive away.

Maybe I am writing another story,
Whose main character isn't you,
Instead, you're just an old lost glory,
With whom I don't know what to do.

Maybe when I finally push away,
And wipe you from my swirling thoughts,
It is then that to you I'll say,
How I wasted all my shots.

But, maybe, it just may be,
I will realize another thing,
My power is strong in me,
I am my own queen and king.

Maybe love is supposed to walk away,
Maybe it just came to teach you how to live,
Maybe love just couldn't stay,
Without teaching you to forgive.

HELLO

Hello dear society,
I wanted to tell you a few things, if I may,
First, let's give you an applause,
For all the dreams you keep at bay.

Let's smile and shake hands together,
While you whisper behind our backs,
Let us worry on our own,
How to fix each of our cracks.

Let us talk and laugh about good memories,
Forgetting the wishes we once had,
And the thought that we could reach the stars,
Before you told us we were mad.

Let's admire you for your courage,
How you stand up for everyone,
Let's praise your loving big heart,
For always judging none.

Let's sit, talk and make a toast, dearest society,
To all the rules you have refined,
To all the upside-down smiles as well,
And all the hopes that you've made blind.

I MISS

I miss what I felt,
When I used to be young
I miss the faded ceiling
Where all my dreams hung

I miss the innocence
Not having a facade
The power of honesty
That in me they find so odd

I miss the sounds I heard
When no one else noticed or cared
Like the brushing of a leaf
Falling into my tangled hair

I miss the laughter I had
That in full force would explode
And now has become a simple smile
That doesn't let my story be told

I miss the joy I used to find
In such small and daily things
Like the morning sun in my face
Or a bird fluttering its wings

But most of all, I miss how easy
It was my feelings to forget
'Cause now it seems that my whole life
I'll forever be in their debt

SUMMER DAY

The sun is shining through the windows
On a beautiful summer day
As my feelings welcome me with open arms
Saying: "Please, enjoy your stay"

There's nothing better than freedom
Running around and then starting to pray
That the present never ends
On this beautiful summer day

And I know fall will come soon
And then the leaves on the ground will lay
But I'll always keep the memories
Of this beautiful summer day

So give me something to remember
For instance, a kiss would be okay
Because then I'd never dare forget
This beautiful, beautiful summer day

5 THINGS I LIKE ABOUT YOU

Sometimes I prefer to sit by myself
Read a book, or just be
Thinking quietly in my mind
What could you possibly like about me

Do you like the way I look
And the colour of my hair
Or do you love the way I think
And the way I always care?

I don't really know what you see
Truth be told
But I do know this
My memory of you will never grow old

There are endless things I like about you
Such as the way you talk
Or the way your blue eyes sparkle
When towards me you walk

Maybe it's that you understand me
In ways no one ever could
Or how you make me break the rules
Ones that without you, I never would

I could go on and on
Writing verses and talking about you
But what I like the most of all
Is how you say: "I love you, too"

DAMAGED

Look at what we've made
Of this ever changing blue sphere
It seems incomparable
To what was before we were here

We remain indifferent to the damage
While the Earth's always in motion
But it doesn't take one look anymore
To notice what color's the ocean

And what about the animals
Those who came and went
What right do we have to kill them
Or simply to cause them torment?

What about the nature
That we're slowly taking down
Just remember the O2 we're losing
While we cut a tree from the ground

But I'll let you all in a little secret
There's so much we can do
Starting from the little daily things
To the bigger most important ones, too

And let's all get together and work
To make this world a better home
So in the future all our children
Will love this Earth with their heart and bone

YOU

I never knew him so well
I only saw him from afar
His soul was a mystery to me
But then, so was his heart

It felt so weird to feel this way
For someone, a stranger to me
But I failed to let go
So I just let it be

Thinking it'd pass with time
My feelings hidden away
But they didn't leave at all
It seemed they were there to stay

They say that once in a lifetime
You meet the other half of your soul
And until you both are reunited
None of you will ever feel whole

And then, I suddenly realized
That I had met him, too
And though at the time I didn't know
It just so happened to be you.

I WILL

Before I start painting my own path, first, I will go and apologize to everyone I've wronged
I will run to my parents and thank them for every action I forgot
Then, I will tell my brother to be his unique, awesome, amazing self because that's who he is; I will tell him to never believe anyone who says otherwise
I will go to my best friends and let them know that I love them; that I really hope they get what they're looking for in this thing we call life
And then, I will leave, I will go to the ends of the Earth until I find what my heart is searching; I will memorize every step I take and every breath I breathe that's leading me there
Every song I sing and every person who gave me love, I will let no one stop me from getting what I want
When I place all my bets in one's table, it means I won't give up so easily on them; and if they make me laugh hard enough that I start to cough, I will cherish them even more
I will walk through life with my arms in front of me
That way, even though the shards of pain will cut my hands, the most beautiful unexpected things will fall right into them
I long for the day I get to call a place my own house
When I get there, I won't stop until I make it a home
And if anybody tries to stop me from being the best self I could possibly be
I will dismiss them, knowing their words aren't worth a damn to me.

TRUE LOVE

It can find you when you're lost
You would never know it came
You can lose it all so suddenly
Then nothing will ever be the same

It will raise you high above
The most powerful drug there is
You will write stories with its feeling
Like a poet does with his

You will feel like you can reach the stars
Like there's no one stronger than you
You will feel so powerful
Like there's nothing you can't do

It can open up your heart
And embrace it with strong hands
It will give you so much more
Than all the oceans and all the lands

It will show you many wonders
You never thought could exist
It will wave one last time
Before it fades away in the mist

We are all meant to feel it
Once in all our lifetimes
You will never stop chasing it
Until the last clock ends its chimes

It can grow up with you
Or with you it can grow old

But know you won't ever forget true love
For it is a flame that never grows cold.

TO ALL THE PEOPLE I CARE ABOUT

To all the people I care about,
Please remember this goodbye,
And even though I'm going now,
There's no reason for you to cry.

I am forging down my path,
Following every single dream of mine,
I'm not trying to rush anything,
I just want to cross that line.

Without hesitation,
I am taking what I want,
The present is all that matters to me,
My past isn't allowed to haunt.

I am caring about the small things,
About every kind gesture I receive,
About every person who wishes me good,
And about every other I forgive.

I am loving with all my heart,
I am living with all my soul,
And I promise, in all my life,
I have never felt so whole.

SOMEWHERE

Somewhere on the other side of the world,
A girl is hating her existence,
While her mother cooks dinner downstairs,
And her father, he watches the news.
Somewhere, a doctor drowns himself in alcohol,
After failing to save another's life,

But he doesn't understand,
That maybe he's losing his own.
Somewhere, a homeless prays,
That a good heart comes to save him,
He has no idea...
...the good hearts need the most saving.
There are so many lost souls in this world,
And, oh, it's a pity they can't find themselves,
Wishing that someday all this would end,
Cause it's so hard to have to pretend.

Giggles and Tears by Sigi

_____I_____

I'm the type of person who rarely gives up
Who cares only about the important things
Who has suffered less pain than any other
But yet wishes they would leave her to flutter her wings

I'm the kind of girl that can't get broken
For I always have gotten away
I never fail to see the good in people
Whom others think cannot be saved

I believe there's something beautiful everywhere I go
I believe there's something miraculous in everything
I see I just don't quite know what to say anymore
When people aren't trying to find my key

I understand that my flaws don't define me
And I never let them get inside my head
But sometimes it becomes really hard
When everyone probably thinks I'm mad

I love being able to try new things
Routine has always sounded boring to me
I prefer to live in the real world
With my body dangling at the edge of my fantasy

Helping others gives me a kind of joy
That nobody could really explain
It brings me a happiness so sincere
When I relieve someone of their pain

My body may be smaller than others'
But my heart so big it could never fit in my hand

And with it I'll give them all the love they think they don't deserve

And show them that some things aren't meant to just e...

THE STORY OF ME

There once was a little baby,
Whose eyes wandered everywhere,
But as I started to grow older,
Not everyone understood that curious stare.

At first, I sought guidance from my parents,
Those who had been there the most,
But the more I opened up to them,
The more I figured I was lost.

"Perhaps my friends can help",
I told myself after some years,
Thinking because of the same age,
They might share my biggest fears.

But since this brought me no peace,
I realised something then,
You can't always find solace in others,
Sometimes all it takes is picking up a pen.

So I wrote and wrote and wrote,
About the things that made me smile,
About the melodies I danced,
And books that kidnapped me, for a while.

I wrote about the people,
Who were there in times of need,
I even wrote about the ones,
Who never really did.

Writing helped me figure that,
I was never meant to stay,

And suddenly I didn't feel so lost,
For I was already on my way.

WHY

Why should I do it? Why should I try? Can't I just run away?

But they're all just holding me back,
Telling me the best thing to do is stay.

Know that all people get tired one day,
Sick of these secrets and lies,
You can see it in their bones and skin,
But most of all you can see it in their eyes.

"Trust me," they say,
"I know what's best for you,"
But deep inside we all know,
That what they're saying is not true.

And though they tell me to hold on,
'Cause if I didn't I'd fall so low,
I believe that by myself I could fly,
So I just close my eyes and let go...

IT

It can heal you from your pain
It can take you far away
It can release you from your chains
And it always asks if you're okay

It will care about you like no other
It will always be your rock
You will hold on to it and not bother
About the society's never ending mock

It can give you so much happiness
You'd never known you could possess
It can gift you a tenderness
You'll always feel that sweet caress

It will trust in you when no one seems
Support in everything that you do
You can tell it your hopes and dreams
And it will make them reality for you

I have only heard it from others, though I just really wish
I would feel it, too
And maybe deep down I did know,
That I would feel true love,

Did you?

WHERE

Where am I gonna go
In all this big wide blue sphere

I don't think I'll ever know
What is my worth down here

So I lay my head down low
And don't let anyone near

I haven't had enough time to grow
I still don't see what I hold dear

But I know I gotta start slow
So let's lead this life with joy and not fear.

CHANCE

What did you do to my eyes
Please tell me, no more disguise
What did you do to my heart
I think it has made a restart

What did you do to my soul
All of a sudden, it felt so whole
What did you do to my mind
This feeling is one of a kind

Just one look and my feet melt in the ground
My eyes stop whenever you are around
I can't help myself it seems so clear
I am different when you are near

Standing still as you start to speak
My heart feels heavy, my knees are weak
My thoughts dance in melodies I've yet to know
And this unknown feeling begins to grow

How can I go on without you
If you're in my mind what can I do
I keep on telling myself, you see
That now, you are nothing to me

But I know, that's a lie
When I look into your deep blue eyes
Turn around please, at me still glance
Let's give this love one last chance

IF I SHOULD GO AWAY

If I should go away and not still stay
Would I remember you just like before
Or would I think about you no more
As my heart and soul keep turning gray

All my bare truth in front of you I lay
Forget the lies my childish heart once wore,
And every oath to you, my love, I swore,
For they were deeds of hearts so young and gay.

My love is certain as the sky has stars,
But there is still no end to my young sun,
And when I look up there's nothing but light.

It feels as though I keep on chasing cars,
My feet never get tired from the run,
As I wait for the mistress of the night.

FAMILY

They are my light in this sea full of darkness,
In this world, they are the ones I trust the most,
Adding fuel so my fire shines with brightness,
When I set the sails, I know they're waving at the coast.

They are a safe place for me to rely on,
When I feel drained and my feet can't hold,
They bring me strength when my power is gone,
And they shower me with warmth when it gets too cold.

Everyday they teach me how to love,
How to care and how to give,
How to turn ravens into doves,
How to wait and how to live.

They let me grow as a wildflower,
Shaping myself along the way,
Never did they need to lock me in a tower,
They know I'll come back every time I go astray.

They give me honesty and never lie,
Even when I want them too,
They tell me to always reach for the sky,
When I feel there's nothing I can do.

They make our house feel like a home,
And now I see it, oh so clearly,
Even when the whole world I roam,
My family will always be what I hold most dearly.

SUNFLOWER

You were my summer's last sunflower
But not in any ways the least, you know
We started it wrong and ended it right
Fall has come and now you have to go

This season faded and with it so did you
We let go before we held on
One second you were right here
And then the other you were gone

And now I long for those three months
More than you will ever do
For we were something that could've been
A love so magnificent and the most true

YOU CAN'T

You can't silence my mind,
No matter how much you try,
For it is a storm within itself,
That will never seem to die.

You can't bring down my soul,
Like you've brought many others before,
For I've always been strong,
And I've never stopped at the shore.

I have constellations of galaxies inside,
And compared to them, the universe is so small,
The stars are still young in there,
It's gonna be long before any of them fall.

At this moment, right here,
You can't hold me in,
For I am slowly ascending,
Unhurried, going for the win.

I KNOW WHO I AM

I know who I am
I found my peace within
I don't define myself
In the confines of my skin
I don't let my worth be judged
By the limits of your mind
I don't compare myself to anyone
For my truth only I can find
I don't hold on to something
Unless it's worth fighting for
I always strive to do good
Wishing I could do more
I would never want to blend in
Or live in somebody else's lie
'Cause we only have one short life
Unlike the stars in the night sky
And I will admit up to a fault
I can't help myself but be proud
That I never let society stop me
That to broken hearts I never bowed
I never got held up for someone
Who was not worth holding on to
And as soon as I realized that
I simply let go and flew
Because I knew, know, and always will
Who I was, am and will be
And though I can't be others in this world I am the only one who can be me.

PHOENIX

Deep in this old and torn town
Where I too often go
There's a girl who can't be held down
'Cause she's a fire burning bright and slow

And this girl has been to hell
And never the same when she came back
Before, she thought what she was missing
What memories in the future she'd lack

And though she did what they wanted her to do
She never got to think about what she, herself, wants
She never got to say all her truths
And that her forever will taunt

That girl never thought she was beautiful
'Cause she never was looked at that way
She never saw herself in the mirror
'Cause she left before she could stay

This young girl has returned now
Stronger and all they can think about
Though she may say there's no beauty within her
They all know there's no beauty without.

ALMOST

Giggles and Tears by Sigi

Once, somebody told them:
"You're not gonna get if you don't do
And if you're not sure of what to say
Remember that not everything starts with you"

They always thought they were too scared
That they were gonna ruin this whole thing
So keeping their words to the shore
Seemed better than breaking their heart strings

What they wouldn't understand
Even though tomorrow they will
Is that you can't keep going forward
If your body is standing still

You can't give it another chance
If you haven't even tried
If you haven't given it life
You can't say that it just died

We don't say it, but tomorrow will come too soon
And then regrets will be all you can hold
Regrets of how you never even stepped up
Of how your thoughts you never truly told

Because there exists nothing harder
Than this word so common and known
"Almost" is something that never fades
And in your mind it's forever shown
They didn't know that at the time
But now it still didn't seem too late
So they decided to step up now
Or else themselves they'd always hate

Giggles and Tears by Sigi

But then in the middle of the way
Their hearts cracked open and made a turning
And they realized that their flames were too bright
For them to let others stop their burning

So they turned away slowly
Without leaving any trace of them there
They decided to not want others to know
About how they'd smile and how they'd care
And with no luck they said their silent goodbye

Thinking it was the worse they'd ever give
Their last thought was: "We almost made it,
We almost loved,
we almost lived."

I CAN

Giggles and Tears by Sigi

Once, a thought popped in my head,
And only in that instant did I know,
That I am the author of my own story,
And I can write my happiness as I go.

I can choose any path my heart desires,
I can see every corner of the Earth,
I can make a home anywhere I like,
And only I can determine my worth.

I can give love with all my heart,
Even though highly it would cost,
Because I know if I don't get anything back,
It is actually they who have lost.

I can weave words into poetry,
In my imperfect unique way,
I will spread them out in the ocean,
And I'll never keep them at bay.

I can make my voice be heard,
Or can I be silent to the rows that don't matter at all,
I can do anything I want,
Before time hangs up on my last call.

OUR SOULS

Giggles and Tears by Sigi

How strange would it be
If I told you my life's not about me
How strange would you find
For someone who seems to have lost their mind
To believe that all our lives' dear hidden treasure
Is something that goes beyond time and measure
Is something that doesn't come from our pockets' inhibitions
Or our 195 countries' demolitions
It comes from a little something that can't be found
It can't be paid and it has no sound
You can't weigh it in kilos, pounds, or tons
'Cause only in your veins it deeply runs
Until you believe it exists you can't see
What it profoundly means to just be
It is within your body, either you have it or you don't
Some days you will need it, some others you won't
It's that feeling that you have when you help without a price
When you make an effort and you just throw the dice
It's that genuine good heart that makes the world go round
And although others pull it under the water it cannot be drowned
It's that hope you have that never dies
It's where your deepest desire always lies
It's what makes your days feel whole
It's your never fading soul
I do believe there's a higher power out there
But it's not something that the sky may bear
In our souls, we each are the God of ourselves
Only us, and no one else.

HOME

Giggles and Tears by Sigi

This small blue sphere has many beautiful things,
It has the sky, with the birds, fluttering their wings,
It has the earth, with new buds, popping up every day,
It has the sea, either kissing the shoreline or simply walking away.

This Earth that we have lived in for so long,
Has beautiful creatures, both weak and strong,
It has incredible minds that can move mountains,
But it also has some people that can rise and fall like fountains.

Here, are many distances that I'd like to go,
And here, there are many things that I'm yet to know,
Here, is lots of air that hasn't yet reached my lungs,
And here, are many good songs I haven't already sung.

But, if you look deep inside you will see,
There is a place for each of us, even you and me,
We have been there many times, or maybe not just yet,
Though sometimes, its existence, we happen to forget.

Out of all the beauties this planet may carry,
Only one can make you so joyful and merry,
And even if the whole world you roam,
There's nothing more divine than a little thing we call our HOME.

GO!

Leave your worries far behind you,
Feel the sweet taste of summer air,
Let the sun warm up your face,
Let the sea breeze mess up your hair.

Dive head first into the ocean,
Don't come up until your lungs can't hold,
Make friends with the birds flying above you,
Never leave your stories untold.

Run as fast as a lion,
Have the strength of an ox,
Stay as loyal as a wolf,
But sometimes as cunning as a fox.

Count the stars in the dark sky,
Listen to the silence of the night,
Fall asleep under the trees,
Then wake up in the morning light.

Go see views you never saw before,
Go do things you never thought you would,
Your time here is still long,
So reach for as many stars as you could.

HOW CAN YOU SAY

Giggles and Tears by Sigi

How can you say you know me
When you haven't seen within
When your judgment's only based
On the softness of my skin

How can you say you own me
When my person was never for sale
And whatever part of me you may have
It's not bigger than the tip of my nail

Because I'm an ever-changing sea
With waves that come and go
Which can wash your memory away
When? You'll never know

You think you can describe me
By using one word or two
But I assure you I'm more than that
I'm a never-ending book

And maybe you're stronger
And your life is more complicated than mine
But don't for a second believe
That gives you the right to define

WHERE WILL I GO

Where will I go
I do not know
I am not counting the hours
I'll take it slow
Go against the flow
And run in a field full of flowers

Summer is near
That's why we can hear
The birds oh so joyful song
Come on with me
Happy let's make thee
Come on and with me sing along

Let's go out and play
Not sit in and stay
For out there are wonderful things
Let's smile at each other
About worries not bother
Let's take off and flutter our wings

The nature's delirious
The night is mysterious
Together the most perfect pair
Laying on the grass
Feeling the stars' sweet caress
Knowing neither when nor where.

I AM ENTERING A NEW LAND

Giggles and Tears by Sigi

I am entering a new land
Where nature's melody is all you can hear
Where white oak trees proudly stand
And other souls are far from near

An old wooden bridge has made this place her home
But it's been a long time since any have stepped there
I am the first that has come here to roam
And breathe this soft and green air

The tears are falling endlessly
It seems they never go into that puddle
They wet the cold carved stones carelessly
Their cry has made even me befuddle.

This forest I'm talking about
Is a magical, mystical ground
Where beautiful flowers may sprout
And you can hear the silence of nature's immortal sound.

THE EARLY MORNING HAS COME

The early morning has come,
In this frozen far away land
Here there is no drought
Nor any color of the sand

Snow has covered everything
Even the tops of the highest mountains, too
I wonder what's behind them
Or, dare I say, who?

Reflecting above the water
At least those parts that aren't covered by ice
The sun is the king of this whole scene
A scene you can never see twice

And though the sea is freezing cold
And ice patterns hide its being
I simply wish I could dive in there
From the world completely fleeing.

AN OLD RED TORN ARMCHAIR

Giggles and Tears by Sigi

An old red torn armchair stands quietly on the grass
The grass is covered by a vivid green
The green can't surpass the sky
With a blue that's never been seen

The clouds make figures dancing on air
And the lake reflects the afternoon sun
I wish I could sit in that red armchair for days
Where I'd think about everything and everyone

I would look closely to the horizon
That at first sight seems so far away
I would soak my feet in the water
Then, I would run around and play.

I WRITE THIS

Giggles and Tears by Sigi

I write this to say my goodbyes
Because now I am flying away
I am chasing the horizon
For the rest of my infinite days

I am running towards the sun
Even after it sets I'm not gonna hold
I know that my friends are shielding me
From this world when the times are cold

I feel the splashes of salt on my feet
As I leave my shoes behind and run like the wind
On my face I feel the warm heat
At last, to their walls I'm no longer pinned

I am in the search of myself
Going against each wave that comes to me
I am slowly rising from the ground
And letting go of reality

I've always been a human running,
A human fighting, a human seeing,
Now I'm the sea, the earth, the wind, the fire,
But most of all, I'm a human being.

TIME

As the past fades away
New memories are made
Memories that you think are forever
But soon they too will fade

The present is slipping through our fingers
And nothing ever seems to last
As everything we ever do
Disappears into the past

With our eyes squinted looking far
We search yet we cannot find
What we're desperately looking for
A hope that has made us blind

Our souls are pushed forward slowly
As the non stopping clock of life can never die
Oh imagine how wonderful it would be
A world where we have an infinity of a thing called time

ONE DAY

And maybe one day we will meet again
I'll be a woman and you'll be a man
Then the whole world would still go round
And you to me would always be bound

'Cause every night I lay in my bed and think
How shallow would be the ocean if we wouldn't sink
How high above would be the blue sky
If we wouldn't feel the clouds as they cry

I never meant for me to hurt your heart
I never meant to tear us apart
But if you'd just look deep inside you would see
If only one thing's forever, that is you and me

And I know that we don't need to find our other halves
'Cause we complete our own selves, we do
But I never said I needed you to be here
I only said that I wanted you to

THE DREAM

Giggles and Tears by Sigi

I find solace in the songs I sing
In times of need they are my friends
I fall in love with all the stars
That shine in the sky that never ends

As it rises above the mountains
The sun gives a stop to all my dreams
I struggle to remember what they were
But they run fast away like river streams

Then I go to sleep again
Hoping they will come back to me
And I dream of a strange new world
Where anything you want, you can be

This dream makes me think deeply
About the world we live in everyday
And it makes me wonder what if we'd leave
And into my dream world we'd stay

We have a lot of sadness in here
That our hearts sometimes can't bear
What if it washes away
Once we go breathe a different air?

In my dream, the oceans were on the sky
And the grey clouds under the sea
And the waves that kissed the shore
Were the only rain I would see

I MAY FORGET

My mind can't remember it all
I may forget the sun rays on my face
I may forget the waves brushing my feet
Or the way the stars shine up in space

I may forget the smell of flowers
When they are blooming in the spring air
And I may forget the cold in my hands
When I run in the snow without a care

I may forget the hugs that I give
The "thank you"s and "sorry"s of everyday
I may forget the times that I smile
And the small white lies that I say

But for all of my young days
Deep in my heart I always knew
That as long as I can love
I will always remember you

THE SECOND LOVE

Giggles and Tears by Sigi

It was never love at first sight
He didn't think she was anything but a girl
Someone who loves herself
More than anyone in the world

Loving her crept up on him
Unexpectedly he swept it away
Thinking it would never happen
Unless she too had something to say

She made him laugh so hard
That sometimes he couldn't catch his breath
But he made her cry so much
Almost like putting her to death

He was so surprised to meet her
Thought he'd never get the chance
Maybe knowing her was
Just a pure coincidence

And though she may not have been supposed to
To come into his life so soon
Although he's living in the morning
He can't wait to welcome noon.

FROM MY PERSPECTIVE

Giggles and Tears by Sigi

I saw it first, when I was five years old
Or, at least that's the first time I remember I did
On a Disney movie, I think it was a Friday night
I learned what love was as a kid

I saw it in the eyes of the ones that raised me
In the eyes of the ones who were always there
The unconditional love you can have
When you're not afraid to lay all your truths bare

I saw it when I was young
A small little kid in love
Imagine how funny it was
Until all that push came to shove

Since the days when I was young
I haven't seen it again
And I wonder where I will encounter it next
And I wonder when

For I'm sure that something great is yet to come
A grand love I have never felt so far
I know I will see it very soon
And when I do, I will never say au revoir

THE MOST IMPORTANT LESSON

Giggles and Tears by Sigi

We can fall at rock bottom
And we can rise back at the top
We can cry as much as we want
Or we can let not a single tear drop

We can make life be worth it
By wisely using all our time
Or we can stay in bed all day
And then end up with a dime

We can explore the whole world
Or we can only see one place
We can kiss many people
Or we can kiss only one face

We can learn how to love
How to take or how to give
But most important, before we die
We must learn how to live

JUST SO YOU KNOW

Giggles and Tears by Sigi

You can hold the whole world in your hands
But it still wouldn't be enough
You can be very soft inside
Although you're always trying to look tough

You may hold a smile every minute
Every second of every day
You may leave just before getting hurt
Even at the times when you wish to stay

You may keep your mouth shut
Every time they tell you to hush
But their opinions have their own toilets
And you've learned since little that you should flush

You may slam your door at me
Make me trip and make me fall
You may break my heart by showing me love
And then saying you felt nothing at all

You may belittle me
And call me irrelevant in so many ways
But I know that all my life
I shouldn't let some seconds determine all my days

'Cause my soul knows the importance
Of small and beautiful daily things
And no matter what may hurt me
I know it's a temporary sting

THE THIRD WHEEL'S POV

Giggles and Tears by Sigi

They found each other utterly intoxicating
It could be noticed by everyone
They were the only people who didn't see
That their link could never be undone

The way they kept sneaking glances
Even when they knew the other was looking too
Made them so happy and complete
That without each other they just felt blue

They thought themselves insufferable
It was strange how they enjoyed being near
And how they felt like the luckiest people on earth
When their voices were all they could hear

But believe me when I tell you
There is no love bigger than theirs
And to their gravity towards each other
Not even the Sun's compares

THE HIGHER POWER

Giggles and Tears by Sigi

Can you imagine a world without me?
I can't imagine one without you
Can you imagine a place where you don't know
Who I am and what I do?

Cause every time I close my eyes
My heart and mind both say
That if you weren't here, next to me
I'd be damned for all my days

If a song comes out and I listen carefully
They all remind me of you
When I look and you're smiling at me
You don't know what you put me through

There's an energy inside of you
That gives me joy and light
It gives me happiness and it makes
Everything I see look so bright

You can break my heart
And tear apart my soul
You can shatter my mind
But still without you I wouldn't feel whole

So please don't make me go
And please don't let me leave
Call out my name into the crowd
And make me believe

If there is something out there
That has a higher power than we do

Then it's not in the sky or under us
It's the love that gets us through

MY AFFLICTION

I'm tired but I can't sleep
Everyone thinks I'm weak
The Earth pulls at my feet
And I can't hear my heartbeat

I've been this way for too long
I gotta show that I am strong
I think I know where I belong
And I hope that I'm not wrong

I need to stop wasting my time
Chasing without having a dime
I know my future is what I'm
And wanting to know it, isn't a crime

When they ask me I say I'm well
I deny hiding under my shell
They don't know that I once fell
I went through both heaven and hell

PAST LIVES

In all the worlds I've lived before
I've never seen something like this
A place where water comes to the shore
And gives the sand a gentle kiss

Where birds start chirping above the trees
And four-feet buddies run around
I've never seen things like these
In the past worlds where I was bound

And in all the places I never knew
People who came and went so fast
Who in an instant completely grew
Lived their lives and went, at last

For in the worlds I lived before
I was immortal until the end
When I'd slowly slip under their doors
And into a new life I'd ascend

But of all those lives I ever saw
None has ever mattered more
Cause though the sea has that one flaw
We forsake no time before the shore

WHEN I MET LOVE

Love ran me ragged and burned me out
Ignited a fire within and then left me in the drought
Love changed me to the core
So that my tears could never again reach the shore

Love helped me get on my feet
And then kicked me hard on my knees
Love brought me the sweetest high
Only to leave the next day without saying goodbye

Love told me to always be myself
That I should never compare who I am to anyone else
Love kept me warm in times of need
And my heart from the cage it freed

Love knew how to make me cry
Or laugh, or live or how to make me die
It knew how to make my day
And it always knew when to walk away

There's a vague memory of what love felt like
As if I was unceasingly hit by a lightning strike
But no matter what I do to forget
I'll always remember the day that love I met.

THE SECRET OF LIFE

Giggles and Tears by Sigi

When I first made a mistake
I didn't know what wrong could come from it
I was too young to understand its consequences
And when I made the second
I learned to say: "He did it."
Moving from day to day
From hour to hour
From year to year
We all make mistakes
And sometimes, it is as simple to erase as if you hadn't made it in the first place
But then, there are those mistakes that can last for a lifetime and that still
Wouldn't be enough to fade away your guilt
How strange it is to think that we can just blame someone else
And hope that the guilt leaves us and washes the shore of another soul
But that sea always comes to kiss us back
Tell me, when you do something so wrong you can't talk about it to anyone
What do you do?
I'll tell you what I do,
I hope
I hope for the sake of myself and for the sake of others that one day,
I might become a better person
Not for God, not for Satan but for me
For the people that I love and those that want what's best for me

But even that, may not be enough sometimes
Sometimes that guilt eats you from inside

It crawls inside your veins and poisons your blood until you no longer have the will to go on Yet, how fortunate we are to have a second chance at making things right And how strange it is that we are oblivious to that fact
Still, that's what's beautiful about life, though
It doesn't come with erasers,
But you can always flip onto another
page.

THE MIRACLE OF LIFE

Giggles and Tears by Sigi

Once a tree was born from the grass
Far inside the frightening woods
Where no one has ever dared to pass
Because of the darkness that there broods

And inside the darkness the tree grew
With leaves that were so full and green
They gave light like this forest never knew
And made it alive like it never had seen

It gave these woods a will to live
A purpose that seemed heaven-sent
It taught them to share all their beauty
And not cause others torment

Once, when I entered in that place
I felt lost like I'd never been
I was even afraid to touch my face
Fearing it wasn't the same skin

But when I saw that tree
Tucked in a hidden cave deep inside
I had no more desire to flee
For I had finally found a guide

LIVE

Giggles and Tears by Sigi

Fly above the highest mountains
Where the sun kisses the sky
Run across the greenest valleys
And hear your heartbeat passing by

Dig so deep into the ground
That you will find what you once hid
And let the soft grass brush the memories
Of everything that you once did

Dive head first into the deepest oceans
Swim below until your lungs explode
Drive too fast in your hometown highway
Don't stop until you reach the end of the road

Go and break apart all that once built you
Watch as your atoms become one with the air
Show the universe you are not afraid
Of every wonder it gave you to bear

Dream of a place where the grass is greener
Where the flowers are always in bloom
Where the trees reach to infinity
As you strike a match to dispel the gloom

There are moments when we're infinite
When we feel like we're on top
When no one can ever stop us
No matter how many times they mock

And in those exact moments
Life is the best thing you'll ever own

And you'll vow to protect it
With all your heart and all your bones.

MY PROMISE TO YOU

Giggles and Tears by Sigi

I can't promise you all that I am right now
For I haven't had time to search for myself yet
I can't promise that I will always remember
How you made me feel I might one day forget
I can't promise luxury and all that you want
My hands are still too small to hold so much
But they start burning like a supernova
As soon as your hands they touch
I can't promise you my body
And all the pleasures of lust
For I have not learned to control
All that rebel stardust
I can't promise you to be there
Anytime that you need my ear
I can't promise that all the time
You will find me right here
But with all my heart and soul
I will promise you this
That I'll gift you my love
Every time that we kiss
I will give you my mind
And tell you all you can be
I will help open your doors
And discover their key
I will give you my soul
And all the kind words it can birth
I will make you understand
Just how grand it is your worth
I will guide you through your mind
So we can defeat your demons together
And I promise you will learn
How to get up on your own forever
Today I can't promise you
I can give all that you may desire

But I can promise that I'll always be the match
To help you light up your fire

I cannot promise that I
Will give you every part of me
But I promise you that in all of your days
True love is all that you will see

I WANT TO GO ON AN ADVENTURE

Giggles and Tears by Sigi

I want to go on an adventure
With the one I've yet to know
We'll wonder the whole wide world together
Without thinking about tomorrow
We'll swim through oceans that never end
We'll follow the river back where it was born
We'll climb the highest mountains
Until our feet get numb and our clothes get torn
We'll hold hands for the longest hours
And we'll kiss under the moonlit sky
For as long as we're together
Not a moment will pass us by
We'll watch as cities rise and shine
As we welcome the sun at our hotel window
Music, art, culture and love
Will become our own shadow
And as the night will come so fast
We will still be laughing out loud
As we stumble upon a small bar
And we push our way through its crowd
We will drink until our heads get dizzy
For it's only then that we let our hearts grow
When your eyes looking through mine
Devour my today and tomorrow
I want to go on an adventure
With the one I've yet to know
We'll wonder the whole wide world together
Never looking at the ground below

WHAT ARE YOU LOOKING FOR?

If you're looking for time
I cannot give you mine
If you're looking for trust
Mine has crumbled to dust

If it's beauty you seek
It's not to me you should speak
If it's adventure and fun
I'd suggest you'd better run

But if it's something that's found deeper within
Surpassing through air and inside your skin
Reaching in your veins, both body and soul
Believe when I say in me you've found it all

If you're looking for love, compassion and tears
I promise to help you face your most frightening fears
If you're looking for eyes that shine like a child's
Just look at my face, always crippled with smiles

And know that as you look for that love
Which seems to no longer exist
I am also looking for you
In all of this confusing midst

OUR WILDEST DREAMS

Giggles and Tears by Sigi

We all have our wildest dreams
With skies of purple and clouds of blue
Where everything that seems impossible
Inside those dreams it becomes true

We all have our greatest desires
Who and what we want to be
All the people we wish to love
All the places we wish to see

We all know our deepest fears
What scares us until it makes us weak
And we always look for that same cure
The cure that heals these fears, we seek

But do we all not know as well
That all these dreams may not come true
That maybe reality is all that is
Inside the frame of our world's view

Don't we know deep in our hearts
That wishes, they can never be enough
That to get what you want in life
You need to be both brave and tough

And don't we know that all too well
Fear is what keeps us alive
It cannot be cured, nor healed
Because without it we can't survive

We can have all of those dreams
All of those hopes, wishes and fears

But one thing that we should know
You cannot count them by the years

THE ABYSS

Giggles and Tears by Sigi

I am trembling as I stand
At the edge of the abyss
I am shaking, there is nothing
That can scare me more than this

I look down at the bottom
Where uncertainty and fear reign
Hoping that if I fall one day
I can come back up again

And then a face shows up
In that pit far away
Then all I want is just to jump
Just to fall and just to stay

And I'm falling, falling down
Feeling like I'm flying up above
In that thing that we wish for
In that thing that we call love

I regret it not one bit
It has only brought me joy
It has not beaten who I am
It has not played me like a toy

I have not cried and cried for hours
I have not sorrowed in despair
I have only seen the beauties
It births and sprinkles in the air

And though one day I may see
The ugly parts of this abyss

I think about all the good things
As I give in to another kiss

SIMPLE TRUTH

Giggles and Tears by Sigi

Some people are here for a moment
For others a lifetime is not enough
In this world that makes us all feel a bit lonely
When times are too cold and rough

Some people, they leave 'cause they should
Some others because they are scared
Some leave because they are meant to
Our paths were not supposed to be paired

But as people come and go as they do
There's only one who never leaves your side
You might still be looking for that person
As they always have just loved to hide

When things go wrong and it becomes too much
There's only one who will always stay there
No matter how much it will hurt them
No matter if it's more than they can bear

And as you grow and love and live
You will learn one simple truth
This person has always been inside you
It has carried your soul since your youth

You might have thought you'd never find it
That it was a myth made from lost hope
But finding yourself is too true
When you feel you're at the end of your rope

And though people do come and go
Though they leave with no said goodbyes

You should never feel too lonely alone
For that is when you learn how to thrive

IF YOU EVER NEED ME

Giggles and Tears by Sigi

If you ever need me
I will be right here
Holding your hand
And shedding your tears

If you ever need me
I'll come running fast
And wrap my arms around you
So the hurting can pass

If you ever need me
I won't hesitate
I'll leave all my problems
And come to you straight

If you ever need me
If you really do
I'll always be there
Because I-

TOXIC

Giggles and Tears by Sigi

You make me mad every second of every day
All that you do and all that you say
Should show me that the best I can do
Is to simply stay away from you

You make me sad and you make me cry
You make me stop wanting to try
And you break my heart in a thousand parts
Like a glass that is broken in a thousand shards

But whenever I'm down you make me feel high
At times when I'm dead you make me alive
With only one look and only one smile
You make my anger seem always worthwhile

And though this passion might be temporary
It can never be anything close to ordinary
And though I may hate everything that you do
I can't tell myself to stop loving you

ADJUST

Giggles and Tears by Sigi

There are many who feel they aren't enough
In a world where being different is rough
There are many who feel that their worth is too small
There are even those who think it doesn't exist, at all

When the things people say, think and do
Are the exact same opposite of you
There is no need to worry about whether you'll fit in
All you have to do is just go for the win

For there is beauty in the odd and bizarre
If only you showed exactly who you are
You could make your presence on this earth so grand
You could brave all oceans and conquer all lands

And if you ever think that you should just change
To fit in with the ordinary stardust
You should always remember to be you
And the world will simply have to adjust

THE TREE

Giggles and Tears by Sigi

In this world there is a type of tree
That blooms from the seed of a glance
She is showered with warmth and with the power
Of a connection birthed only by chance

This tree should be sprinkled with water
But not too much or else she will drown
Like the tears of a heartbroken daughter
Drowning her soul when she is let down

This tree belongs in the sunlight
Cause the sun never ceases to burn
He helps her grow helps her take flight
He helps her feel and he helps her learn

And as the tree starts to grow older
Her roots become stronger than before
Though her head sways more to her shoulders
She has never been so secure

None of us are here for too long
And the trees are in the same race
But this one tree is so odd
She surpasses both time and space

This tree can grow to infinity
And never gets tired of birthing new leaves
She slowly approaches divinity
Achieving what no one believes

And as this tree follows this path
It cares neither for envy nor hate

It cares only for what it does hath
Which are the keys to the most beautiful gate

REMINDER

You remind me of falling asleep in my
Warm bed after a long and tiring day
Of waking up to a rainy morning
In a not-working Sunday

Of my favorite book when I was a little child
Of a time when I was fearless, brave and wild
Of all the smiles I have received in all my years
Of all the times kindness has wiped away my tears

You remind me of my favorite ice cream flavor
And my favorite sing-along
Of the first poem I ever wrote
Of the first time I knew I was strong

You remind me of all the good things in my world
You remind me how to feel
And though I do not know you yet
All that I know is that this is real

MINE

Giggles and Tears by Sigi

I knew right from the very start
You were a card from a different pack
As I looked into your eyes
And I found them staring back

You took my soul with that light blue
Stole it right from under my nose
And made my heart beat so fast
That I think it always shows

And in those few moments
That we have spent together so far
I have never felt such a connection
Grow so rapid from the start

I do not yet know if I
Feel the way I think I do
But I always find myself smiling
Every time I think about you

Our lives are one big puzzle
And we don't know the pieces we've got
There are people who fit perfectly
And there are those who simply do not

I once thought that for me
Those people would be hard to find
But it seems when you're around
You're the only thing in my mind

I do not reach for my phone
Or lift my eyes up to the ceiling

I do not find a distraction
From the place and from the feeling

I can break your heart you know
And mine is at risk just the same
Every time you make a joke
And every time you say my name

And if you've listened to me talking
I am sure that you have heard
The things that I don't say
In the space between my words

And I hope that you have felt them
The same way that I do
And I hope that you will tell me
When you feel you're ready to

I once thought it was impossible
To be so vulnerable in such short time
But I hope that I'll be yours someday
And someday you will be mine

LOOKING OUT

Giggles and Tears by Sigi

On a Friday evening
When the stars shone bright
We were the ones
That most lit the night
When the flames ignited
From the touch of my hand
We suddenly discovered
Where our hearts land
And we laid our heads
Down in the ground
And we looked at the sky
As the world spun around
Then we stole a glance
From each other's eyes
As this heartwarming feeling
Warmed our hearts by surprise
It grabbed all of my reason
Along with my rational doubts
And it threw them away
Hid them above the clouds
Then you suddenly left
Taking my heart with you
Leaving me alone
With nothing to do
And I stayed anyway
Picked myself up through the years
I embraced my own soul
And wiped away my own tears
And though i am better now
I'm still staring at the starry sky
Hoping for the better days
And looking out for you tonight

FOREVER

Giggles and Tears by Sigi

When your shoulders can't hold
All the weight you need to carry
We will work it out together

When your eyes can't hold
All the tears that are gathering
We will work it out together

When your mind is filled
With sadness, anger and grief
We will work it out together

And when your smile can't seem to disappear
I will laugh with you

When your happiness is infinite
I will be happy for you

We will work it out together
Because even though you may not know it
We are forever

MY FAVORITE

Giggles and Tears by Sigi

I have many favorite things
In this world of laughs and cries
But above everything else
My most favorite are your eyes

They hold specks of stolen sunlight
That always put me in a trance
They are the deepest blue of the ocean
That can drown me with one glance

They hold never-ending emotions
That can burn me with their fire
They hold pain, anger and fear
They hold love, they hold desire

Your eyes can trick me into staying
Even when I say I'm going
They are magnetic in that way
They grab on me without me knowing

And I have always hated the way
Those eyes looked right through my soul
As if I could hide no secrets
From those eyes that searched me whole

But they are still my favorite thing
Because of that singular shine
And I love those eyes even more
When they are looking straight at mine

OFTEN

Often times I have imagined
How my world will come to be
But it changes that much often
Inside the depths of my fantasy

Often times I have just wondered
If my heart's in the right place
And often times have I observed
All the small changes of my face

Will I grow to become good
Or will I stray from the right way
Will I embrace my Lucifer
Will I live the night and sleep the day

I do not yet know my fate
Or where I'm supposed to do
I do not know what I want
What I need I do not know

But I believe that I will find
All that's supposed to belong to me
And until then I needn't worry
All I need is to just be

TO MY FUTURE SOMETHING

When I'm a little older
And a lot more bolder
I will find the key

The key that opens the gate
Of a place where there's no hate
But only love for eternity

I will find the map to my heart
And hopefully have a new start
With you form a new team

A team stronger than all
Where love swallows us whole
And forever is what we will be

Seasons will change with the wind
And the people will come and go
But I will always be there for you
I'm telling you this so you'll know

My love for you will be too deep
Too strong and too warm for my mind
So I'll follow my heart for the first time
And I'll leave all my worries behind

THE CYCLE

Giggles and Tears by Sigi

I have come from far off lands
That nobody has heard of
I have now both feet and hands
I now can hurt and now can love

I am stepping out of my home
And over the comforts inside my fence
All that I am and all that I own
My heart, my soul and all of my sense

And I am walking forward slowly
With every step that I am taking
My path has never seemed so holy
With every rule that I am breaking

My feet are rushing on the ground
Preparing for my biggest fight
Not against those around
But against the day and night

All of a sudden I am running
Towards what I came here for
Though to me life has been cunning
It has always opened another door

But as the end of my run get nearer
And I can hear the cry as I fall
I regret nothing of the life I lived
For I was brave and I stood tall

SIZE TWO

Giggles and Tears by Sigi

Thick or slim
Short or tall
Why does this seem
To matter at all?

Brown or blue eyes
Fair or dark skin
All that really counts
Is who you're within

Big or small nose
Upturned or down
All that you should know
Is that it doesn't count

For you can be the greatest
Person in the world
And still be moved by insecurities
Like all we other girls

Cause they want us to
Find faults in ourselves
It's what they live for
Just like everyone else

But you should know there's beauty
In the imperfections of what we do
And our value's so much more
Than just being a size two

About the author

Sigi is a 16-year-old junior high school student from Albania, a small country in Europe. This is her first collection of poetry which she began writing at only 14 years old.

Despite her interest in writing, she intends of studying biomedicine in college and hopes to one day become a successful scientist.

Sigi has a keen interest in sharing her work with the world so others could enjoy and perhaps relate to her poems. Her passion about reading poetry inspired her to express her feelings and she has not stopped ever since.

Giggles and Tears by Sigi

Copyright © 2020 SIGI

Giggles and Tears

Perspective Press Global Ltd

All rights reserved.

ISBN: 978-1-8380044-2-2

www.ingramcontent.com/pod-product-compliance
Lightning Source LLC
Chambersburg PA
CBHW021443080526
44588CB00009B/667